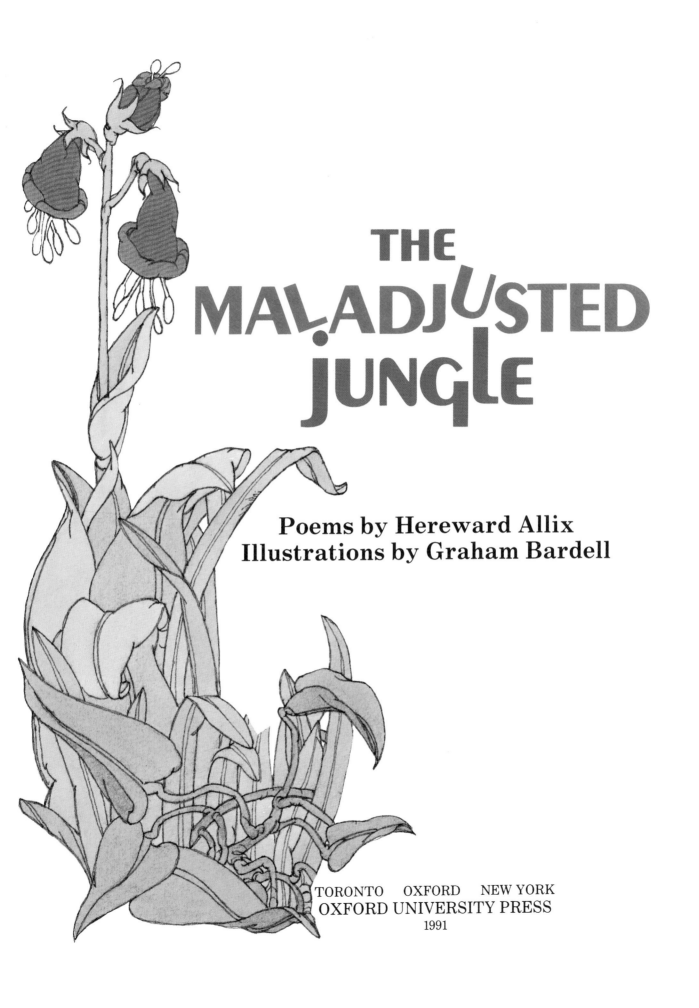

THE MALADJUSTED JUNGLE

Poems by Hereward Allix
Illustrations by Graham Bardell

TORONTO   OXFORD   NEW YORK
OXFORD UNIVERSITY PRESS
1991

For Louise, who began it all.
— H.A.

For Ron and Paul
— G.B.

Peggy

Peggy was a polar bear
    who wanted to be warm.
She hated Arctic temperatures,
    and loathed each winter storm.
She dreamed of waving palm trees,
    blue lagoons and golden sand,
A fantasy her relatives
    just could not understand.

They said, "You have a fine fur coat
    to keep the cold at bay.
A polar bear is what you are,
    and that is what you'll stay!"
But Peg did not appreciate
    her Arctic uniform;
She admitted it was stylish,
    but it wasn't really *warm*.

Besides, there was no comfort
    in that pallid midnight sun,
And sunbathing on icebergs
    simply wasn't any fun.
What she needed, Peg insisted,
    and for which at once she'd plan,
Was a trip to Acapulco,
    Waikiki or Mazatlan.

A friendly travel agent
    made a booking on the spot
To a Caribbean island
    where the sun was always hot.
She got herself a passport,
    and an airline ticket too,
Then one freezing winter evening
    Peg packed up and off she flew.

Her relations, while enjoying
    a refreshing shower of sleet,
Were quite certain she'd expire
    from an overdose of heat.
They said, "She'll never make it!
    She's a goner, that's for sure!"
And they shuddered at the thought
    of that infernal temperature.

Meantime, Peggy was enjoying
    every moment of her trip.
She landed, had her coat shaved off —
    right off, from toe to tip —
Bought a polka-dot bikini,
    changed, and headed for the shore,
Where long, lazy afternoons
    of sun and swimming lay in store.

And Peg has never changed her mind:
    she never will return
To the land of endless nights,
    where only whale-oil lanterns burn.
She says she has no use for poles;
    there's really nothing there.
And she claims to be the first
    and only true UN-polar bear.

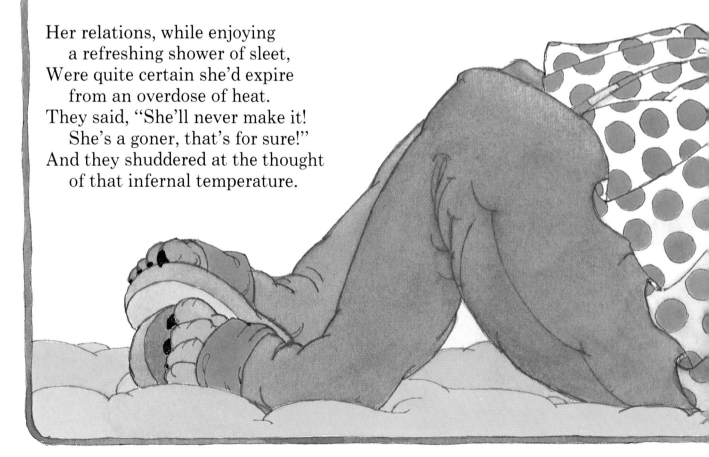

Lily

A leopard cub named Lily
    was unhappy with her spots.
A few might not have mattered,
    but this little cat had lots!
She hoped she would outgrow them —
    but her mother had them too.
And she noticed with despair
    that they got bigger as she grew.

She tried every kind of lotion,
    and used sixty sorts of soap,
But her spots shone all the brighter
    and she almost gave up hope.
So she tried another method,
    and her howls grew even louder
When she found she could not cover up
    those wretched spots with powder.

Then at last she gave up trying
    and resigned herself to fate,
Convinced that with her spotty face
    she'd never get a date.
Till Len, a handsome leopard boy,
    discreetly held her paw
And whispered, "You've the nicest skin
    I think I ever saw."

Now Lily is a mother,
    and she tells her spotty cub
As she gently soaps its silky skin
    while splashing in the tub,
"Be grateful for your assets;
    don't tie yourself in knots.
And whatever else you do, my child,
    don't try to change your spots!"

Katie

Katie was a kingfisher
    who wouldn't eat her fish,
Because she said she found it
    an unappetizing dish.
Her parents were distracted,
    for they couldn't come to terms
With their daughter's most humiliating
    preference for WORMS!

So they plied their infant offspring
    with all sorts of finny food,
Which they themselves had always
    found particularly good.
From stickleback to sturgeon,
    and from herring roe to hake —
But Katie would have none of it
    and screamed for earthworm steak!

Her father had no notion
    how to catch the wily worm,
While her mother viewed its cooking
    with a shudder and a squirm.
But as Katie daily weakened
    and would surely fade away,
They knew that something drastic
    must be done to save the day.

They consulted Dr. Heron,
    a psychologist of note;
He said, "You must not force
    unwanted items down her throat.
To do so is a grave mistake,
    unhealthy and unwise,
So I think it would be better
    if we found a compromise."

The solution he suggested
    was both clever and astute,
And its overall effectiveness
    was never in dispute.
For Katie now looks fatter,
    and as healthy as she feels,
As she downs her daily diet
    of delicious baby eels!

Osbert

I tell of Osbert Ostrich
    and the feathers in his tail.
He made it clearly understood
    those feathers weren't for sale.
But a milliner named Mildred,
    who made ladies' hats galore,
Wanted Osbert's finest feathers
    for her high-class fashion store.

Now Osbert hadn't been to school;
    he wasn't very bright.
He thought that if he couldn't see
    he must be out of sight.
So he went and stuck his silly head
    inside a pile of sand.
And how Mildred got his feathers
    he will never understand.

Vera

Vera was a vulture,
　　sitting on a rock,
Feeling very sad because
　　she had no meat in stock.
Her stomach was *so* empty,
　　and nothing seemed to die,
So Vera had to get along
　　on vegetable pie.

Cecil

Cecil was a centipede
 with fifty legs each side,
Which were to him a source
 of unrestrained and sinful pride.
He delighted in their shapeliness,
 as well as in their number,
And was very proud and boastful
 when he danced the Spanish rumba.

How he teased the other animals,
 and laughed with rude abandon
At those creatures who had only
 two or four good legs to stand on!
When they tried to do the tango
 or the minuet, or such,
He would imitate them meanly —
 only fifty times as much!

His conduct was disgraceful,
 and his manners far from nice;
His mother was ashamed of him,
 and said so once or twice.
He was horribly unpopular,
 but did he care a bit?
Why, no! Upon the contrary,
 he seemed quite proud of it.

One day our Cecil came upon
 a strange and thrilling thing,
A kilted Highland gentleman
 was practising a fling.
And this, of course, the centipede
 had never seen before,
So he sat and watched the Highlander
 from three till half-past four.

When he felt that he had mastered
    every detail of the dance,
Cecil leapt to all his hundred feet
    and thus began to prance —
Heel, toe! Heel, toe! He danced as though
    his hundred feet had wings,
As he executed half-a-hundred
    perfect Highland flings.

The Highlander was very cross
    at Cecil's show-off act —
"It's an insult," he cried bitterly,
    "I'm mad, and that's a fact!"
So, to soothe his indignation,
    and to heal his wounded pride,
Off he went to do more dancing
    on a distant mountainside.

The dance that he selected
    was a celebrated one —
The famous Scottish sword dance,
    very difficult but fun!
He laid the swords upon the ground,
    their blades at angles right,
And his toes tripped in between them
    with the speed of flashing light.

The Highlander was happy then,
  for little did he know
The cunning centipede had found
  a way to watch the show.
He had climbed another mountain
  and was sitting on its slope
To observe the whole performance
  through a borrowed telescope.

Cecil thereupon decided
  he must do this splendid thing
Which was so much more exciting
  than the simple Highland fling.
He would far outshine the Scotsman
  and he'd do it with panache —
Alas, he had no inkling
  he was heading for a crash.

He stole the Scotsman's swords away
  that self-same moonlit night,
And no one saw him do it
  because no one was in sight.
He laid them on the dewy grass
  beneath the shining moon,
And began to dance as lightly
  as a butterfly at noon.

But oh, how slippery is grass
  when hoary with the dew!
He slipped and half his hundred legs
  the gleaming blades sliced through.
Poor Cecil's cup is bitter,
  and he's drained it to the dregs
As he stumbles clumsily around
  on fifty wooden legs!

George

Young George was a giraffe
    who had a very long sore throat.
(He should have had a higher collar
    on his overcoat.)
His tonsils were so swollen
    that his doctor said, "No doubt!
I must send him to the hospital
    to have those tonsils out."

The surgeon took one look
    at that long throat and said, "Oh, heck!
I cannot reach his tonsils;
    they're too far down his neck!"
So George still has his tonsils
    in his gullet so remote,
And his mother had to buy him
    a high-collared overcoat.

Mary

Mary was a mongoose who
    was terrified of snakes.
She knew she ought to kill them,
    but she hadn't what it takes.
Her father and her mother dealt
    with serpents by the score,
While her brothers and her sisters
    made short work of many more.

But Mary had a tender heart;
    besides she could not face
The disturbing feel of snakeskin —
    for a mongoose, that's disgrace!
Her revulsion was a weakness
    Mary never overcame.
And although she often thought she might,
    she didn't die of shame.

Oswald

Oswald was an ocelot,
    a great big furry cat.
His coat was very beautiful,
    and he was proud of that.
But Oswald was, it's sad to say,
    a natural-born worrier,
And his sleep was interrupted
    by bad dreams about a furrier.

This furrier kept shop
    in a most fashionable place,
Where fine ladies came to purchase
    all their luxuries and lace.
His business it was booming,
    and he made a lot of money
Selling Oswald's kith and cousins —
    Oswald found this far from funny.

So he went to see his doctor,
    who'd had psychiatric training,
And who lent a sympathetic ear
    to Oswald's loud complaining.
He soon diagnosed the problem,
    understanding Oswald's plight,
And prescribed a special treatment
    that would cure his nightly fright.

"Next time you dream that dream,"
    he said, "imagine you're right there,
And tell that horrid furrier
    that you're too tough to scare.
Then buy his shop and close it down!"
    And that is how, it seems,
That Oswald overcame his fear
    and had no more bad dreams.

Percy

Percy was a penguin
    with a culinary flair,
A talent, that in penguins
    is comparatively rare.
So it isn't so surprising
    that this clever bird should want
To open up Antarctica's
    most stylish restaurant.

On an isolated iceberg
    in the Bellingshausen Sea
Percy built his place of business,
    with himself as maitre d'.
With crisp white shirt and black bow tie,
    he really looked the part,
While a chef's hat was the symbol
    of his culinary art.

The menu was extensive
    and unquestionably fine,
And each course was complimented
    with a European wine.
From plankton soup with sherry
    to eel steak with Beaujolais
There were treats for every kind of taste,
    and gourmet all the way!

There were octopus' adenoids
    in albatross egg sauce,
And a tantalizing sorbet
    would be served with every course.
There was never any question
    but that Percy did excel
At delicious gourmet cooking.
    It's a shame it didn't sell.

For the average consumer
    on Antarctica's wild shore
Likes his meals uncomplicated.
    Or, to put it bluntly, raw!
So poor Percy soon went bankrupt —
    lost his shirt, as one might say.
He's the only all-black penguin
    ever seen in Biscoe Bay.

Suzie

A little snake named Suzie
  was afflicted with a lisp;
Instead of truly hissing,
  she achieved a sort of "hithphe".
Her childhood was unhappy,
  for she suffered ridicule
From the other little snakelets
  at her kindergarten school.

As Suzie grew, her problems
  were too numerous to tell:
Her crooked fangs in braces,
  and a scaly skin as well!
She felt lonely and discouraged
  as she set about to find
A friend who'd overlook her looks
  and love her for her mind.

Then there came a transformation!
  Suzie shed her blemished skin.
And her fangs came out of braces
  straight and bright as a new pin.
She was slinky and attractive,
  and it all came down to this —
She would carry all before her now
  if only she could HISS!

Suzie took some singing lessons
  from a musical guru,
Who pronounced her voice delightful,
  very strong and sweet and true.
She sang the words of every song
  in tones so clear and crisp
And, incredibly, without the least
  suggestion of a lisp.

Suzie's now a happy adult,
  and a famous opera star.
Her admirers flock to hear her,
  flying in from near and far.
She's among the foremost singers
  and her voice is all the rage
As her hisses ring out brilliantly,
  both on and off the stage.

Cedric

Cedric was a crocodile
    with rows of gnashing teeth;
He had a hard and horny hide,
    on top and underneath.
His tail was long and scaly,
    and his feet were webbed and flat,
And a great grey greasy river
    was his lonely habitat.

He lived by eating people,
    and he ate them one by one,
Digesting them quite peacefully
    while sleeping in the sun.
You could tell that he was happy
    by his beatific smile,
For he was indeed a healthy
    and contented crocodile.

Then one day a river steamer
    with a cargo-load of sweets,
Such as chocolate bars and marshmallows
    and other toothsome treats,
Was wrecked upon a sandbar
    and its cargo split and scattered,
While the crew escaped in lifeboats,
    which was all to them that mattered.

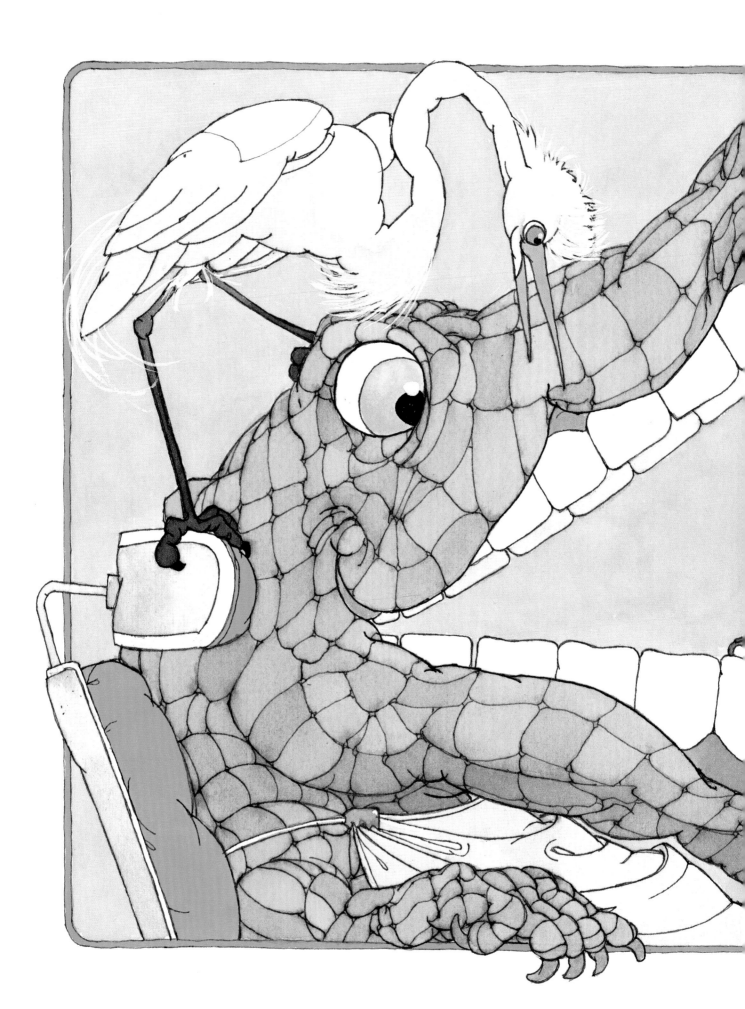

The candy boxes came ashore
    not far from Cedric's lair,
And the crocodile was curious
    to see what might be there.
He sniffed the tempting odours,
    ate a chocolate bar or two,
Then found a pack of spearmint gum
    and settled down to chew.

From that day on good Cedric
    lived exclusively on sweets,
Lost his appetite for people
    and indeed all kinds of meats.
But sad to say, his shining teeth
    had cavities galore,
And when he tried to gnash them
    they all fell out on the floor!

So he went to see a dentist,
    who commanded, "Open wide!"
And discovered with astonishment
    no single tooth inside.
Then he made a set of dentures
    in a crocodilian style,
Which restored his patient's former looks
    and beatific smile.

Now Cedric is quite careful
    of the kind of food he chews,
And if you offer him some gum,
    he's likely to refuse.
He never touches chocolate bars,
    or marshmallows, or such,
But if you give him mincemeat he'll say,
    "Thank you very much!"

The Political Jungle

Zoë was a zebra of
    a most unusual type.
As well as being black and white,
    she wore another stripe.
Her political ambitions
    were Conservative and strong,
For she felt that left-wing animals
    were dangerous and wrong.

So she joined up with the party
    and became a candidate,
In the animal elections
    of her distant jungle state.
She built herself a platform
    and got ready for the fight,
In the absolute conviction
    that Conservative is RIGHT!

Her opponent was a panther
    of distinctly pink persuasion,
Who preached beastly revolution
    upon every occasion.
He growled and roared and ranted,
    and repeatedly he swore
That the zebra was a Fascist,
    And he'd fight her tooth and claw.

Zoë bravely faced the panther
    in a televised debate,
Being certain that his ego
    she could speedily deflate.
But the panther was her equal
    in the verbal cut and thrust,
And she realized that she
    must somehow conquer him or bust!

The panther equally was sure
    that he was going to beat her,
And decided then and there
    that otherwise he'd have to eat her!
So, as polling day came nearer,
    there was tension everywhere,
And at all the jungle meetings
    there was not a seat to spare.

The herbivores and carnivores
    opposed each others' choice.
The candidates themselves
    were in especially good voice.
"We'll devour them!" yelled the panther.
    "We'll masticate their bones!"
"We'll kick their silly teeth in!"
    Zoë screeched in strident tones.

When the ballots were collected,
    and the counting was all done,
The rivals waited, confident
    that each of them had won.
But when the TV screen displayed
    the count for all to see,
Both contestants were defeated
    by a Liberal chimpanzee.

Oxford University Press, 70 Wynford Drive, Don Mills, Ontario, M3C 1J9

Toronto   Oxford   New York   Delhi   Bombay   Calcutta   Madras   Karachi
Petaling Jaya   Singapore   Hong Kong   Tokyo   Nairobi   Dar es Salaam
Cape Town   Melbourne   Auckland

and associated companies in
Berlin   Ibadan

Canadian Cataloguing in Publication Data

Allix, Hereward
The maladjusted jungle

Poems.
ISBN 0-19-540781-4

1. Animals — Juvenile poetry.   I. Bardell, Graham.
II. Title.

PS8551.L55M3 1991   jC811'.54   C90-093984-2
PZ8.3.A55Ma 1991

Oxford is a trademark of Oxford University Press
1 2 3 4 - 4 3 2 1
Printed in Hong Kong